MOBIL MARKETING

AND

SOCIAL MEDIA

INCREASES

PROFITS

Dr. Gene Ritchey

Sequoia

The information presented in this book is based on worldwide research and personal experience of the author, and is true and complete to the best of the author's knowledge. However, this book is intended only as an informative guide for those people wishing to know more about this field of knowledge. The information presented in this book should be available to the public, so they can make informed choices.

With life comes privileges and responsibilities, and with both come risks. No matter what you do there are risks. The author and the publisher are not responsible for any adverse effects or consequences resulting from the use of any of the information in this book. Please consult qualified professionals. Using the informed knowledge of others is a sign of wisdom.

MOBILE MARKETING and SOCIAL MEDIA INCREASES PROFITS

Dr. Gene Ritchey, 2011.   FIRST EDITION

ISBN – 13: 978-1466202153
ISBN – 10: 1466202157

CONTENTS

Acknowledgment   ix

This book is dedicated to Sydney R. Ritchey,
my granddaughter and special friend.
She nourishes me and gives my heart wings
through her endless Love, Joy, and Happiness. ❦

ACKNOWLEDGMENT

It seems like every book project takes on a life of its own. I always start with a planned schedule, but something always happens and my schedule seems to evaporate. Writing a book always takes longer than planned or expected. It seems the book's schedule has a mind of its own, and my desired schedule takes a backseat. It seems there is an intentional effort afoot to change and reorganize the fruits of my sprit; persistence and patience are the fruits which are getting the most attention. For all this, I am most grateful. Through these transformations I have grown and in addition I have been nurtured by some very kind, caring, and loving people. These are without question — angels whose participation was essential for me and for bringing this book into reality.

I will be thankful forever for the help of Beverly Thorp, whose brilliant vision and understanding provided me with inspiration and caring. There are many, many other people who helped and supported my efforts. This list is very long and I cannot hope to name them, but they deserve my sincere appreciation and thanks. However, there are some who have to be identified. It is a privilege to offer my sincere thanks to Beverly Thorp, Sydney Ritchey, and Linda Hagedorn. Each of these individuals has helped in extra-ordinary ways. I appreciate their continuous help and support.

My special thanks to everyone for making me look good! 🐾

MOBILE MARKETING
and
SOCIAL MEDIA

INCREASE

PROFITS

Chapter 1

A Brief History

The success of every business enterprise depends mainly on its effective marketing campaign in determining how many people it is able to reach. Before the internet, if they needed a product or services, they found companies by using the yellow pages. Every person read the newspaper if they wanted to keep abreast of news developments, or looked if there were any new promotions for certain products. Later, people were content in watching television or just listening to the radio.

It was almost certain every individual would read newspapers and magazines, listen to the radio, and/or watch television. It was common, when people walked along the street an individual would pass out flyers. If there was any message to be sent to consumers, it was done through print ads or news media. Companies set a budget for their marketing strategy. Businesses with larger budgets benefitted the most, since they can use advertisements and billboards more often, by printing a lot of flyers or print bigger ads in newspapers and magazines.

In the 1950s, the forms of entertainment for most households were then confined to watching (black and white) television and listening to radio. While tuning-in to their favorite programs, people had to contend with the commercials, which interrupt their viewing and listening pleasure. Households commonly would find their mailbox stuffed with ads (called junk mail), as well as contend with door-to-door salesmen. Marketing strategies then were more of a "personalized" approach, which was quite tedious and costly for the company, and usually annoying for the consumer.

In the 1970s, the use of the telephone proved to be a big step forward in the marketing. These strategists opened a new field called a "telemarketing." Since most people had a telephone at home, companies tried to take advantage of this fact by engaging the services of "telemarketer" to get in touch with each household. Unfortunately, some consumers did not appreciate this idea since calls coincidentally came when the family was sitting down for dinner, or when you were taking a shower. Hence, instead of listening to a fabulous sales message, which the salesman had prepared, the salesman was usually greeted by an angry individual or someone who simply slammed the phone down. The result, the company's marketing mission failed.

The internet soon paved its way in the 1990s and marked the demise of old marketing methods and strategies. At about the same time, computers entered the playing field. Any small business with a computer, a good internet connection, and a web-design could give large companies a run for their money. Businesses can now set up their own web pages and reach a much larger audience. The larger the audience, the better it would be for the business. People who hear of sites with many visitors are curious, curious enough to check it out on their own and they would naturally browse through it. With all of the new visitors, the website owner can expect at least half of new visitors would become customers.

A very large percentage of the population has now stopped reading newspapers, because they can get the latest news faster online. For some people, this is a welcome change as it rids them of some clutter by not having to set old newspapers (even though they can be recycled) outside. This also eliminates the problem of getting their hands dirty due to the newspaper ink and having to handle the old newspapers.

A lot more people are watching television than ever before. Some of these people have switched to cable television. Most people still take pleasure in listening to the radio, especially in their cars. The result of this new shift, yellow pages, newspapers, and magazines are slowly dying. With new items like notebooks, iPods, and mp3 players, people now have the opportunity to read and listen to their own personal selections and not have to surf station to station looking for the song which they like. As for junk mail, it is still filling our mail boxes. We see nowadays junk mail in another form. It now comes as email in our personal inbox. The internet has proved to be a modern approach to marketing.

By the year 2010, the most popular (and least expensive) marketing strategy was through mobile phones and the use of social networking and "tweeting." All businesses now have to do is modify their website, so it can be read on mobile devices, create their own fan page, and entice people, customers and potential customers, to interact with these businesses. This way, businesses can easily update their customers ("followers") with their latest promotions, newest products, and service.

Businesses need to consider a great percentage of their customer base is comprised of young adults who have found it a "must" to tweet every now and then, or simply to check in on social networking sites. Businesses have their work cut out for them. Businesses have to engage and emerge themselves into social marketing or they will die a slow and painful death. By businesses using social marketing they let their customers come to them, by stirring interest in order to sustain their purchases, "endorsements," and continued "liking." It is important to remember, social marketing is not free. Social marketing just like yellow page advertising, newspaper and magazine advertising, and internet marketing, costs money. Social marketing is an ingenious and innovative way of promoting your business and making it known globally.

As we can see, old school marketing methods have slowly found themselves out of place with the modern age of technology. While there may only be a handful of diehards who will opt to stick with the old marketing methods. However, forward-looking companies, the ones which will grow and prosper in the coming months and years, have to see how things are/have changed and move their company's marketing efforts to adjust and embrace these changes. On the practical side, companies have to do what is good for business. Consumers who are into the latest trends would probably endorse businesses and products which are more "in" with the times, because it means they are keeping up with technological advancements. Also, old school marketing strategies cannot simply reach out globally and is usually limited to a certain country or locality, unlike the internet where there is a global marketing presence. ❦

Chapter 2

There is a Need for a Traditional Website

Most companies are aware if they want to expand their business, they have to have their own website. It doesn't matter if the business has no intention of going globally with their product or service, even though it would not hurt to do so. Customers and people within their local community find it impressive and more convenient if a business has its own website, because they get to know about the business, about their products or services, and if and when they have special promotions or offers.

The primary purpose of a company's website is to introduce the company, and lay out their products and/or services. Some companies present online order forms, so customers can order the company's products online. There are companies who provide details on the nearest office or store who offer or carry their products. What is more important, websites also provide contact information where customers or potential customers can contact the business with their questions or concerns. It is also important for business to have an email service on their website.

People want to do business with companies with whom they feel safe and secure. They also like to go to a company where they can easily get in contact with the company should they have any problems. It is natural for people to check if a business is hard to deal with, even after the sale. In other words, customer relations and support plays a very big and important role in any business. Some businesses put some dazzling designs on their websites in order to impress the people. We must not lose sight of the fact in the end, business boils down to the basic simple website, which are user-friendly, provide value, and customer service. Customers today know, they do not have to contend or put up with businesses who complicate matters and make life difficult.

The point is people want to gain access to a website, which can easily provide what they want, because there are instances when the complicated websites end up providing false or even misleading information. Is this an effective marketing strategy? Certainly not. It not only confuses the customer, but it leaves him grumbling and empty-handed. How many people in this world would go back to a company where they had an unpleasant experience?

Small business owners are usually more successful when it comes to establishing these regular and traditional websites because they usually want to go straight to the point in making their product known and do not want to beat around the bush.

They know how important it is to establish some sort of communication or contact with their customers, which is the reason why email addresses and good customer service are provided. This actually serves as the cyber "mailbox" of the company where businesses can check in daily to see if there are any questions from potential customers. People always check on good customer support services or see how fast a business responds to questions or complaints. Customers want to make sure companies do not shy away from their customers and are still there when customers need them. This is the same way companies need their customers to place orders and to promote their business.

Websites are now the latest marketing strategies being implemented in the world. Today, businesses cannot afford to be without a website, unless they want to be out done by the competition. It is practically a game of trying to maximize exposure on the internet without appearing to be pesky or annoying. Websites may seem impressive but then the question is, did they achieve their primary purpose and get the job done? Some websites are flashy but users end up getting confused because they did not understand the products and services being offered. This is why traditional websites are useful, because they send a clear message of their purpose and signals the company is ready to do business. Maintaining a website is a modest cost, but then in the business world, this is just another marketing cost.

In fact, website designs and technology by themselves are constantly changing and improving. If we thought it was static, then we should think again because something has just modernized and changed the marketing world.

With the constantly changing world of internet technology, people can learn to design their own website and change it whenever they want, but the question comes up, "Is this a good use of your time?" Though it may sound easy and impressive, some business owners may find this annoying and disturbing. Regular websites may appear frigid, but business owners do not want to waste their precious time in familiarizing themselves with the newest or latest website software.

Email comes in handy, because angry or disgruntle customers would surely flood the company inbox with numerous complaints. Sticking to a regular and traditional website design is a more user-friendly approach. However, they will surely gain customer loyalty and gratitude, because it can and will be interpreted, the company values their customers. Furthermore, since most companies now adhere to a modernized approach, sticking to a regular or traditional website may later turn out to be a blessing in disguise, since the company which uses it effectively can easily stand out from the rest. It is just a concept of who offers the best service and/or products to its customers. It is not about who comes up with the flashiest or most dazzling website. Sometimes, sticking to the traditional and regular websites are the best, as they cause lesser headaches and lesser confusion, thus, entailing lesser problems for the business owners. ❦

Chapter 3

Route to Mobile Websites

When the internet first made its way into this world, people enjoyed the benefit which was given through their own computers. Those websites were simple, they had standard form, and they were not very classy. The internet did not have the advanced tools or features we have today. Marketing strategists were fascinated with the idea of having to promote their business on the internet, but some people could not decide what to put on their websites. So, they put a myriad of things on it with the idea of sustaining the viewer's interest and attention. The problem with these websites was people could not find what they were looking for or wanted. In this fast-paced world, where time is of the essence for many individuals, these people will surely find this annoying and irritating, since most people want their information in a flash, if not sooner.

When people wanted to get in touch with someone, they were initially ecstatic since they can connect with their loved ones and send messages instantly. This in effect was doing away with the "snail mail" – the U. S. Postal Service. Naturally, most people welcomed this concept with open arms and tried to learn the basics of computer typing so they can send their all-important email which their acquaintances would receive in a matter of seconds. People had to have a computer at home, or probably visit a local library or an internet café to get online. This was a big hassle for a lot of people.

Today, access to the internet is not confined to personal computers or laptops, because people can now easily connect to the internet through their mobile phones. Advanced settings and special features are available on every cell phone model to suit the user's convenience and needs.

Wherever we may be, no matter what time of the day or night it is, the internet can now be easily accessed with just literally a cell phone in your hands. Companies may have foreseen the distinct possibility people will do away with personal computers and just use their own cell phones when they want to connect with the internet. Why wouldn't they? People see no need to sit down and turn on their laptops or personal computers, and wait for it to properly boot so they can connect to the internet. Cell phones have now been designed where emails can be sent directly to it and we can search the internet for anything we can imagine. Cost-wise, having a cell phone which can do what a computer can do, is far cheaper to buy and maintain.

To keep up with the times, mobile phone applications were slowly developed and introduced. When compared to website browsing on regular computers, some find it more convenient to access the web through their mobile phones, because the information provided by mobile websites is less complicated and more precise. Considering this viewpoint is much more restricted and compact. Websites accessed through mobile phones provide simpler designs which the user can easily understand and manage. Thus, businesses now are geared to focus their internet marketing strategies on mobile devices since almost everyone (about 83 percent of the world population) now owns a mobile telephone where they can provide minute-by-minute updates on their status on social networking sites, or where they can give instant "tweets."

Having both a computer and internet access are indicators of advanced technology. Suddenly, here comes another new idea with another advancement in technology which allows access to the internet through mobile phones which people are using every day.

You can't blame companies who are concentrating their efforts in marketing promotions geared to mobile devices. Most people find it amusing to be in constant touch with their friends, and at the same time being able to text someone completely different. Businesses are simply trying to keep up with the current trends.

At the same time, computer users have not dwindled significantly. For some people are always on the road or on the go, it would be a big mistake not to take advantage of this situation, by not promoting products through both mobile devices and traditional websites.

Hence, little by little, people would lessen the use of their computers at home (except for those who are home-base) since they may have been practically surfing the internet the whole day with their mobile phones. Some competitors are now trying to coming up with a website, which will handle both regular internet search visitors and at the same time, offer access through mobile phones to their website. This is not a good solution, because it will only slow down the browser, and in some instances, cause the device to get hung up in never-never land. If this happens, chances are the visitor will not attempt to access the website again because they do not want to experience the hassle of having to shut down and re-power their mobile phones. Hence, to avoid this unfortunate scenario, businesses have to make sure their websites (one for regular internet and one for mobile devices) can easily be accessed through different mobile devices and computers.

Normally, the things we see on mobile websites are the common areas where mobile visitors spend most of their time, because mobile memory space is not large enough to accommodate all those things which we see if we access it directly from our computers. Since mobile phones are practically tiny computers which fit into our pocket, it is no surprise why anti-virus programs have also been developed to guard against system crashes (Yes, this also happens to mobile devices.).

Basically, businesses are capitalizing on the precious seconds spent on the internet when people tweet, send email messages, download music or videos, upload photos or videos, or simply by surfing. Why should companies confine themselves to those who get to access the internet from their own computers when they can tap the growing market of mobile users? It is for this reason new applications and programs are constantly being developed to make it more convenient for people to access the internet from their mobile devices. If people can experience and see for themselves the efficiency of their services and how user-friendly it is to access their website, then this is, by far, a milestone achieved in their marketing strategy. ❦

Chapter 4

Mobile Marketing

Introduction

People usually keep their mobile phones with them as a primary means of communication with the rest of the world. For many people, it is impossible to imagine life without a cell phone in hand or pocket. This is the main concept and driving force behind mobile marketing.

What do you think is actually mobile marketing? If you have searched "mobile marketing" on Google in 2002-2003, you would have gotten something related to marketing using ads on cars and trucks. Surprised? Yes, but now this concept has been totally changed.

Now what do you think is mobile marketing? Here is the answer. Mobile marketing is a promotional activity done by different brands by delivering their advertisements and promotions on cell phones and other handheld devices. It is a new way to present products and services to customers. There are numerous activities involved in mobile marketing like:

- Mobile website owners are paid for showing display ads.

- Text messaging such as SMS (Short message services) and MMS (Multimedia services) are sent to mobile phones.

- Marketing through mobile applications, etc.

Who gets the maximum benefit from mobile marketing?

- Bars
- Restaurants
- Golf courses
- Casinos
- Doctors/Dentists
- Real estate, etc.
- Any business big or small

The following chart[1] showing how different marketing methods have changed; mobile content shows a big increase.

Social Marketing

Social marketing is the use of commercial marketing activities to influence human behavior in order to improve the health and social welfare.

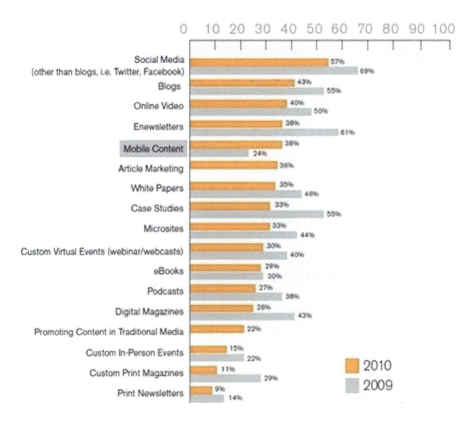

Marketing Changes in 2009 & 2010

Graph 4.1

To practice social marketing, you just need to keep some things in mind:

Know your audience – You must understand the type of audience needed to target. You must understand the reason behind why your audience is not doing the things you actually want.

Take clear action – You should plan your actions seriously. Only then will you be able to highlight awareness among people.

Offer exchange – Offer an exchange to your audience for modifying an old behavior and accepting a new one. Research and get to know what will motivate people the most. This way you can appeal to your audience correctly to help you achieve your dream.

Competition is always there.

With correct social marketing, you can surely increase sales and get improved results.

Social Media Marketing

Social media marketing is related to social marketing. It is a method of marketing using social networking sites like Facebook, Twitter, YouTube, Google Plus, Orkut, etc. This strategy of marketing is simple as you just need to create an account and promote your products and/or services. Also, you can interact on a much more personalized and dynamic level as compared to traditional marketing. A lot of people keep on updating and searching for new things on social networking websites and some people spend most of the whole day searching the internet and texting.

It is also simple to implement with just a little effort, as the promotion is automated. Social media marketing helps sales by increasing or establishing your business' activity on the internet in the following ways:

- Traffic through website
- Tracking of sales and conversion
- Ad exposure and page views
- Broader customer reach through business development

Social media marketing and mobile marketing

Now you must be thinking why these two terms are included? What is the relationship between Social media and mobile marketing?

The fact is these two terms, Social media and mobile marketing, have a deep relationship. We have already seen England's Royal Wedding use these two terms. Through mobile marketing, people around the world were able to see the wedding in seconds. With the advent of 3G and 4G networks, people have started using the internet more, on their mobile phones and keeping themselves updated in social events through social network websites. This is the trick related to mobile marketing.

Today, what companies do is keep their advertisement of their products and services on social networking websites. The companies create profiles and ads to promote their products and services and they are displayed by others. People surfing internet and networking websites on mobile phones, mostly, see those ads and click on it or Tweet, to tell their friends what they have seen. Some even get influenced and buy the company's products and services. Companies even send the link to their profiles through SMS's on mobile phones. This is one of the main reason people use the internet today. Mobile phone usage is increasing day-by-day, which is actually great news for businesses whether they are online or offline.

The sad thing is many companies, especially small business owners, ignore this potentially lucrative marketing strategy. The fact is, social media and marketing on mobile devices is basically the same as any other field of marketing, except this is a new channel of marketing your products and services in a less formal and friendlier way. You get the opportunity to be in front of your audience at the time when they are actually considering purchasing a product or service like yours. This strategy is very lucrative and connects you with the audience in such a manner you have never imagined and this audience is one actually interested in your products and services. This is the best way to promote business and increase profits.

Small businesses fail without mobile marketing

If you search on the internet, you will find 85 percent of small businesses fail. There are many reasons for it, but the most common and most important was lack of marketing, and today it is mobile marketing.

People go for mobile marketing because it reaches the whole world. Your small business could become a big business in just one month because there are numerous people searching for the offers you are making. So, if you do not follow mobile marketing, your business will not be exposed in front of the whole world. Rather, it will just be exposed in your city or street and this means it also takes a lot longer. With mobile marketing you contact millions of people without paying millions. There is no need to send expensive letters, postcards, etc., to inform potential customers about your latest offers.

Mobile marketing helps by displaying a small business in front of the whole world without much effort which ultimately helps in increasing profits. Who knows, you could start making a profit overnight!

Small businesses which do not follow the marketing method outlined above, actually die a very slow death. These type of businesses work in the beginning and only in their city and neighborhood, but slowly instead of getting profitable, they start losing money and ultimately die.

No doubt, small business owners keep marketing programs going for their business, but how many cities or potential customers will they be able to reach? It is impossible for them to create a business name outside their city and if they make it, then forget about outside their country. They cannot do it without internet or mobile marketing, as these are the only avenues available with potential customers at any time of the day or night. Once they receive a message about your company and if they are interested, they will definitely check the website and your products and services. There is no shortage of an audience interested in your business, your products, or services.

To make a long story short; without mobile marketing, business is only confined to their city or street.

Look at the statistics of US Mobile Ad Spending[2] from 2009 and projected to 2014. See the unbelievable percentage of increase each year – 30%, 79%, 48%, 36%, 36%, and 25%.

See how the spending on mobile ads is increasing and this only because of the drastic results mobile marketing is giving.

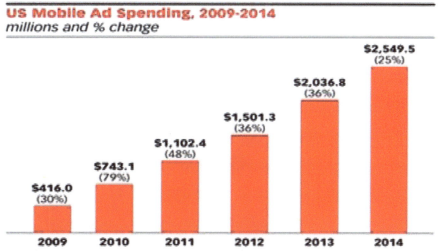

Graph 4.2

US Mobile Ad Spending, 2009 – 2014

Components of mobile marketing

There are numerous components of mobile marketing you can use to promote your business. Some of the most common components are:

- **SMS (messaging/texting)** – Attract the customers through your SMS messages. You can contact a bulk message company which sends SMS to different phone numbers or you can ask people to opt-in to your text messaging list. This is really helpful as people keep their mobile phones with them day-in and day-out.

- **MMS (Multi-media messaging)** – It is almost the same as SMS except for just one difference: MMS contains pictures and/or video. This component helps in displaying the pictures of your products.

- **Mobile Internet** – Advertise your website address and pull customers to your website, through Quick Response code.

- **Mobile applications** – List your application in the mobile and other application stores. Use push mails to market your applications.

- **Mobile content** – Try pulling customers to your website by using content such as images, videos and other downloadable links. This is an Option for mobile friendly websites.

- **Banner advertising** – Pull your customers by placing ads in mobile friendly banners. Make the banners as attractive as possible.

- **Voice message** – Pulling customers using automated voice message delivery. This type of system calls on the cell phone and gives the desired message.

The above components are the most important components for marketing using mobile phones/devices. These are actually successful and give much more profits as compared to other methods of marketing. ❦

Chapter 5

Mobile Marketing for Small Businesses

Mobile marketing helps small businesses

Once there were millions of people, who only dreamt of becoming an entrepreneur, but now, the internet has enabled thousands of people to start or expand their small business with a click of the mouse. Mobile marketing is a great help for small businesses. Look how it can expand a small business and increased their profits:

- **New market** – Mobile advertising is a new concept and there are very few companies which are using this strategy to promote their business. Studies have shown 20% of mobile users say mobile advertisements are actually very acceptable. It is a way you get to know about new products and services just by sitting at home.

- **Large Market** – Millions of text messages are sent and received every day. People prefer using cell phones to view mobile ads as compared to newspapers, magazine, and/or radio.

- **Quick response** – People usually keep their cell phones with them day in and day out and they read at least 97% of text messages received, as compared to email which is about 27%. So, small business can easily contact them and send their advertisements and offers which customers can easily redeem using QR Code, coupons, or their website.

- **Targeted audience** – By using cell phone marketing, you can easily find customers who are actually interested in your products and services. You can also determine who has redeemed your coupon, etc.

- **Passing on** – When you send advertisements on the cell phone of a person:
  (1) A message is saved in the cell phone which the customer can check any time;
  (2) The business number you attach with the advertisement is saved in the phone book of

the person so he/she can easily forward the number to the interested customers.

• **Return on investment is high** – The cost of sending messages on cell phones is really less, almost free, but the profits you get are really high. This means, with a really low investment, you can potentially make high profits. This is the magic of mobile marketing.

Keep in mind; miracles still happen and this is no exception. Miracles can happen with you with the help of mobile marketing.

Mobile Marketing used to get old customers to return

Almost everyone, about 83.33%, in the world today owns a mobile phone which they carry wherever they go. Naturally, mobile applications are being developed since applications being used in regular computers are not practical for use in mobile phones. Companies are slowly shifting their attention to Mobile Marketing to take advantage of the growing population base of mobile users. People love to "tweet" and make blow-by-blow updates on their status on social networking sites. These are only some of the individuals who have benefitted from mobile internet access.

Below is a chart showing how Small Businesses Use of Marketing Tools:[3]

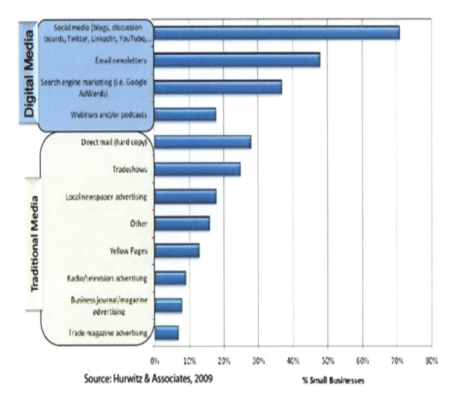

Small Business Use of Marketing Tools

Source: Hurwitz & Associates, 2009

% Small Businesses

Graph 5.1

Can mobile marketing lure-back its old customers? Well, old customers would surely be in for a surprise when they receive messages on their mobile phones from a company they formerly dealt with in the past. Companies can effectively use their past

34

customer base to rebuild old relationships. Old customers usually get what they want to hear when they receive messages on their mobile phones. If people are not impressed with the messages they receive, they can just as easily delete it.

In the case of old customers, companies have a distinct advantage: they know what their customers want and expect, and more or less, they have an idea of what to tell them. It would be a good idea to do a little background checking and analyze why these customers strayed away from the business in the first place and what prompted them to shift loyalties. The good part which would come out of this is when the customer receives the message, the first thing which will come to mind is what the company has to say. A past customer would certainly be more open (97%) to read the text message instead of deleting it. The first step is taken. It is now a question if the company can sustain the interest of the customer by choosing the right words which can help renew his interest. Companies who use mobile marketing, but fail to do their background homework literally face a blank wall when potential customers whom they target do not even bother reading their messages. In short, the messages they compose do not even get to see the light of day. At least with an old customer, companies find comfort and profit as some of their old customers are curious enough to check out on what they have to offer.

Old customers would normally feel flattered as they think the companies went the extra mile in reaching out to them and personally contacting them on their mobile phones, probably unaware of the fact it is nothing more than a devious and efficient marketing strategy to lure old customers back to a business relationship. Retracing those steps and avoiding those words which could trigger what prompted the customer to leave in the first place is the best strategy. Simply put, companies who want to use mobile marketing to attract its customers must do their homework. Otherwise, a single misstep could push the customer away instead of enticing them to return. Customers have to be given a very good reason why they should enjoy the company's products or services. It is a simple strategy of appealing to what the customer likes to do, and other businesses do not have this information. The point is, when businesses have this information, they should use it wisely and to their advantage.

Old customers are no different from other potential customers when it comes to mobile marketing. They also get annoyed in constantly receiving messages which they later delete from their inbox. The first few words and lines are the most important, this is why every word counts. There is an old rule-of-thumb – "You have 8 seconds to capture their attention." If the first line is unable to sustain the interest of the person, then we can very well expect the next few seconds the message will simply dissolve into thin air. In the case of old customers, it is simply a matter of doing a little bit more convincing on why they should return and reacquaint themselves with the company's products and services. As mentioned earlier, with old customers, they have the plus factor of having the message opened and read. The next few steps will then prove to be crucial in determining whether or not the message was successful enough to convince the old customer to return.

The best thing to do, aside from doing a little background investigation, is to choose words which can help the person remember the good experiences they had with the company. If there were untold incidents, all customers need reassurances the company is on standby to answer all their needs and problems should they arise. Is mobile marketing getting too intrusive on the old customer's privacy? Intrusive or not, all marketing strategies, whether traditional or new, have one goal in mind: to entice the customer to order and make sales. It may be treated as intrusive, but then, if marketing strategies are not aggressive enough, how can businesses expect to thrive and flourish in this dog-eat-dog world?

Since most people are using mobile phones nowadays, there can be no better way to get their attention than by using those gadgets which they have on hand and are using most of the time – their mobile phones. Actually, mobile marketing is like the old telemarketing schemes where people call us at home. This time around, messages are initially sent, and calls are made later. To lure an old customer, don't be too pesky; it may drive them away instead of luring them back.

Mobile Marketing used to attract new customers

The best news about mobile marketing is small businesses do not have to dedicate a lot of time and money to reap good profits. See how mobile marketing is actually used to attract new customers:

- **Text Messages** – This is the most simple and effective technique. Suppose you have started a new restaurant and now you want to promote it. The first step to attract new customers is to send restaurant information, menus, and other data via mobile text message along with the contact information. Will they read it? Definitely. Everyone wants to try new restaurants. This is true for other businesses. Each needs to send product and services information about your company with contact information to promote your business.

- **Surveys using text** – People will actually spend time to give you their opinions about your products and services. This is because they want improvements and want to help. Companies can conduct a text poll in return for perks, by asking for their opinion on items. This is an effective strategy to promote a business as well as improve existing products.

- **Coupon sending** – You can attract customers by sending text with coupons which they can redeem easily. Give discounts and gifts, they work really well. Normally, coupons are sent using simple text messages. Today, the use of MMS coupons in increasing.

- **Use Bulk SMS service** – Bulk SMS service sends SMS ads to thousands of people. Book your ad with these service providers and see the magic and see how customers will get attracted to your business.

- **Mobile friendly website** – The trend of using internet on a mobile phone is increasing day-by-day, so it is really important your business' website should be updated and is capable of being viewed on mobile devices, so mobile customers can easily navigate your website anytime.

- **Mobile applications** – Mobile applications are in a great demand especially among younger mobile users.

To attract customers, just create a mobile application with the name and link of your business in it. If you do not want to create one, then opt for an existing application. This will help your customers to link to your mobile website, Facebook, or Twitter accounts.

These are the most preferred and highest profit building tactics ever used to attract new customers. ❦

Chapter 6

Yep Text

What is Yep Text?

Yep Text is an advanced text message service used in mobile marketing which enables business owners to connect customers with just a single word.

There are numerous small business owners who have used mobile marketing but failed, because they did not have an appropriate knowledge and understanding about how to implement this marketing strategy.

Yep Text is here now. It allows business owners to connect to their existing and would be customers by sending text messages online by using Yep Text message service or by the business owner themselves.

There is no doubt text messaging is a big help for small business to increase their access to their existing customers and would be customers. If you are planning to start a business, there is no easier or better marketing method to tell the world you are now open for business, than Yep Text. It helps existing businesses move their business along faster. It is actually a simple marketing method anybody can utilize to promote any type of business.

Most business owners have questions floating around in their head: Is this a good marketing method for my business? Is mobile marketing a good marketing strategy or is it just hype? Is it expensive? How do I start something like this?

It is critically important. Each business owner gets their head around each of their own internal questions and feel comfortable with their answers.

Before Yep Text, mobile marketing was just a dream for business owners. Yep Text created such a simple and straight-to-the-point method it made mobile marketing possible.

The best part is Yep Text is cell phone compatible software and ease of use.

YEP texting help small businesses

Today, almost every person carries a cellphone as their basic means of communication, so they receive and read SMS containing promotional message, discount offers, coupons, and etc. With just about a hundred characters you get the opportunity to have a personal contact with thousands of people and encourage them to try your products and services.

More than 50 percent of people who own a cellphone use text message as a means of communication. This is what helps small businesses. With so many people using text message service, Yep Text creation was such a brilliant, unique, and rare idea.

Mobile marketing is done in a personal way. It easily increases the chances of a successful marketing program and a chance of big profits in no time.

It is also important to use Yep Text effectively to get the desired results. Consider the space given to contact the audience to promote your business. You just get a limited space and it is important you use this space effectively. So design your text message efficiently so it attracts the maximum number of customers. Make it simple so people can and will remember it.

Yep Text is the best way to generate leads. When you send a text message to different people like college students, housewives, etc., you immediately start making them aware of your business and this helps to promote your business better and faster. You will notice the difference between a customer filled day and a low customer turnout day. Yep Texts easily attract customers by using it to send offers, promotions, and discounts.

You have to be fast and effective with your text messages, as your competition is strong. So, in your first message to the people, do send them an invitation to have a look at your store. You can also offer gifts on the first day or their first visit. Keep the communication lines open between you and your potential customers by sending coupons and other promotions.

Once people start receiving your messages and visit your business, they will buy your products and services. They will then start forwarding your SMS to their family and friends. I mean, they start spreading the word about your business which is actually helpful as people trust other people's referrals and testimonials. In just about a week, you will start to notice an increase in the number of customers coming into your business.

Marketing methods are constantly changing and you add this to the rapidly changing technology in business, it is easy to understand why so many small businesses feel overwhelmed and hire internet and mobile marketing companies and consultants. However, the bottom line is:

- Businesses need to take advantage of all of the changes going on around them and their business.

- Its important businesses implement these changes into their business, such as taking advantage of Yep Text and other marketing methods.

Here are some creative ideas to spread your Yep Text:

- Use a poster to spread your word. Write your Yep Word and paste the poster on the window, walls, etc., offering a free gift.
- Make the customers aware of the deals they will get by joining your mailing list.
- When you run ads don't forget adding your Yep Word and the free gift they will get by messaging.
- Put SMS codes on business cards so people can easily save it in their phone book.
- Use television and radio to spread your Yep Word.
- Use social networking sites to promote your Yep Word and business.

Find any place where there are a lot of eyeballs, then try promoting your Yep Word there. ❦

Chapter 7

QR Codes

What are QR Codes and why they are used?

Everybody knows to keep a website in the first ten search engine rankings you have to keep it updated according to Google's rules. Updates can be of different type. It can be blogs, new offers, coupons, etc. on the website. All you need to do is to keep adding new material, so when the search engines' spiders visit your website it finds it alive with the new material. This is a real challenge for website owners and they use all possible strategies to keep the website alive.

There is something new for you, which can benefit your business. Look at the following image:

Figure 7.1

What do you think it is? It is actually a QR code.

QR is the abbreviation of Quick Response which means these codes can be easily and quickly read by a cell phone. In Japan and other parts of the world, QR codes are very common. These codes are basically used to pick-up information and make it readable on a cell phone. You will soon find QR codes on and in everything newspapers, magazines, websites, and commercial products. When read by a cell phone, it can give you information about anything a particular business, a phone number, an address, or a part number. Suppose, you see a person wearing a T-shirt with QR code on it, then it is possible you will find out information about the person through the code.

Sometimes you also get a URL of the website. When you click the URL, you get the home webpage. You can get anything in the code. You can even embed almost anything.

Today, QR codes are replacing barcode because QR code can store much more data, sometimes hundreds or even thousands times more data. The best part is you can scan this code anytime and anywhere using your mobile phone.

The question keeps coming up, how can a cell phone read a QR code? Actually, to make a cell phone read a QR code you have to install a QR code reader in your cell phone's memory, but a camera is a necessary and an integral part of the phone ability to scan the code. It normally only takes a minute to install this software.

To generate a code on your own, you need to use a code generator tool. There are numerous tools available on the internet like close-up with Google's new QR code generator.

Still, confused? Ok, lets look at an example. Here is a Business Card[4] with a QR code on it.

Susan Enzenhofer

TEC-IT

Wagnerstrasse 6
4400 Steyr - Austria
http://www.tec-it.com
office@tec-it.com
T +43 7252 72720
F +43 7252 72720-77

Figure 7.2

Notice: you see a funny looking square of something. It's a code. It's a graphic. This graphic's name is a QR code. The information inside this particular code is the same information printed on the business card including name, address, website address, and contact details. Now, you must be thinking, what is the use of a QR code if the information is written there anyway?

Believe me; it is actually a great value. By scanning this code, you automatically add the information written on the card to your cell phone. The information will be saved in the contact details in your cell phone. Not only this, if the code has a URL address, then the scan will link the user direct to the URL address.

It is a great help for businesses, as they can place the code in their ads, promotional material, and website. The search engine sees you have added new images and material to your website and list it at the top. Today, very few people are using this code, but those who are using them are considered people of high tech knowledge. This is a great thing to open the doors for conversation, sales, and profits. This is another way actually expand your presence on the internet by mobile marketing.

You can use QR codes for your business in numerous ways. One way is to create a code for every product or service available on your website. Place the code at the side of the product with all the details in the code. This is useful as people can easily read the code and save it in their mobile phones. You can add these codes in any print devices like coupons, product details, YouTube videos, etc.

QR Codes in social media

If you have a good approach to the customers in social media, then it is really easy for you to keep in touch with those customers just because of QR codes. Once people have made a purchase, it is quite possible they will come back to your business to buy more products. QR codes make it really easy for them to come back to your business or website to do business. The best part is people have a direct and fast method to reach your company or website. It makes it easier for these people to make instant buying decisions.

A glance at how QR code is generated

To generate a QR code in Google or with any other QR code generator, all you need to do is open the webpage where you will see a text bar to paste in the information you want included into the QR code. Remember, any information can be put into a QR code.

Sometimes, you may want to direct people to a particular webpage where you are offering a discount or a special promotion. It may turn out the webpage has a long URL address, which can be directly included into your QR code or you may want to shorten it to use in your text message as well as you QR code.

There are several different websites which convert long URL addresses to short URLs, such as Google, Bitly, Tinyurl, and others. If you go to http://goo.gl/, Google will shorten your URL. Here is an example using Google's URL shortener.

http://goo.gl/

Now put in any URL you want to shorten. Here in this example we are using the long URL http:// www.etondigital.com/google-url-shortener-offers-qr-code-generator-as-bonus-very-nice/ . After putting this URL in the text box, you click shorten. Here is the screen shot.

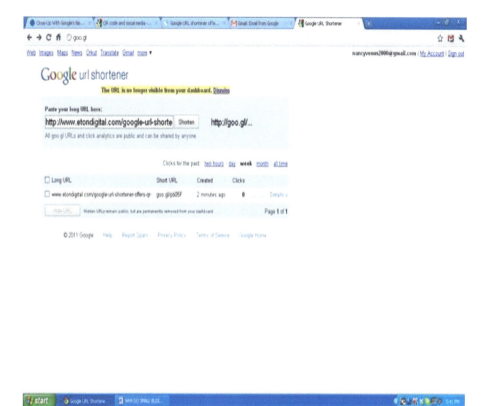

Figure 7.3

Automatically in the window next to shorten, will appear the shortened URL.

http://goo.gl/JCvi

This URL can then be put into a text message or in a QR code.

Creating a QR code is about as difficult as getting a shorter URL. There are several websites who create QR code. If you go to Google's Chart API at:

http://createqrcode.appspot.com/

You can create a QR code. In the above example we use the URL address of:

http://www.etondigital.com/google-url-shortener-offers-qr-code-generator-as-bonus-very-nice/ and if we put this URL or http://goo.gl/JCvi or anything else into the "Text to embed in QR Code" box and click "Create QR Code" button the following QR code is created.

Figure 7.4

This is the code generated of the website www.etondigital.com/google-url-shortener-offers-qr-code-generator-as-bonus-very-nice/. Now you can copy the QR code and paste it wherever you can save it.

Following Chart[5] shows the percentage usage of QR code in each field:

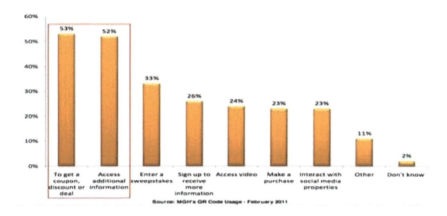

Chart 7.5

Chapter 8

Social Media

What is social media?

Social Media is made up of two words 'Social' and 'Media'. So it is better if we frame the definition by breaking social media. Media is something used to communicate with the whole group of people like on TV, on Radio, in Newspapers, in Magazines, etc. Social media is basically communicating using a media network. This means you not only provide ads for promotion of your business, but also you may interact with the media's audience at the same time interact or at a different time. You can ask anything in this interaction like opinion about your products, services, voting for your article, etc.

What use to happen is, people were just able to watch or listen to something on TV or radio or read a newspaper, but it was impossible for them to give their immediate opinion about the products and services. This type of problem is solved by social media.

Here are some famous examples of social media websites:

Social Networking – Small businesses can create a business account in different social networking sites like Facebook and promote their products and services. This helps in interacting with different people, including existing customers, on the networking sites. This helps promote a small business.

Social News – Using social news people can vote on articles, products, services, etc. They can also add their comments.

Video sharing and photo sites – Businesses can promote their business by sharing photos and/or videos like sharing product photos and demonstrating the products.

Wikipedia – Use wiki to promote website by interacting using different articles and images.

There are many other websites under the social media umbrella. Basically all those websites which gives you the opportunity to interact with other people comes under social media.

Social media is important for small businesses

Social media is a great help for small businesses to gain exposure within their markets. It is good for attracting people by showing the products and services and to increase traffic to their website. Considering the importance of social media, Australian consumers have rejected companies who do not have an online social media presence. Soon this trend will be copied or followed around the whole world.

The first and the most common reason why small businesses indulge in social media is this method is inexpensive and effective. Most businesses, small or large, do not have a big enough budgets to put on marketing and promotion campaigns in multiple medias. Social media helps a lot in keeping your products and services in front of the whole world. Social networking sites like Facebook and twitter are the best way to promote your products and services. Just create a business account in all social networking sites (account creation is free) and see the magic.

If you search on the internet, you will find 60% of the companies who have an online social media presence showed positive impact on their business. This does not mean the left over 40% are dead. These companies just showed neutral results. You can make the results more effective by including other things like SMS, MMS, etc.

The best part about social media is there is no need of a professional marketing guy to promote your business. Any normal person with the knowledge of internet and social sites can do it! All you need to do it is just dedicate time and know how to text and keep your profiles updated. Sounds easy, but it takes time, knowledge, and planning. This is why a large number of businesses hire outside mobile social media marketing consultants to manage to run and maintain their programs.

So, it is really important you should take social media marketing strategies seriously to actually gain higher profits from your business. Just have a look at how marketers utilized Social Media[6] in 2010:

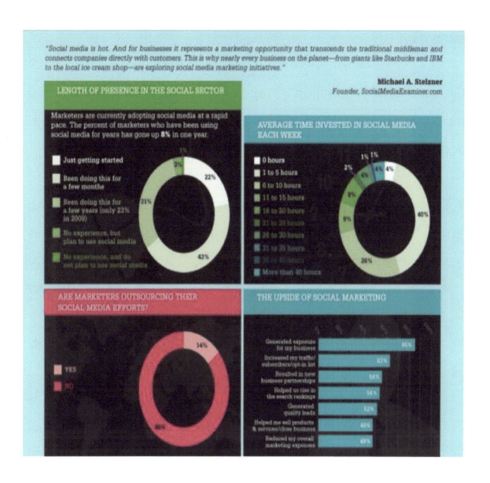

Graph 8.1

How do you use social media effectively for small business?

The use of social media is increasing like crazy. In 2010, the use of this technology in America doubled from 12% to 24%. Do not get surprised, as this is all because of the social media sites like

LinkedIn, Facebook, Twitter, etc. The number of small businesses using social media to generate revenue is actually increasing each day!!!

Ok, so the main question is, how do these companies use social media to build customers lists and profits? Just have a look at some of the most profit generating ways:

- **Creating Pages on Social Networking Sites** – This is the first and the most important step taken by small business owners to promote their business. They usually prefer the three most famous networking sites: Facebook, Twitter and LinkedIn. Usually business owners prepare a company profile page on these three networking websites.

  To get the best profits from social networking sites it is recommended you keep it updated. Some businesses just set a profile page and forget. This does not work. Treat your social media profile as an interactive platform to interact with existing customers and build new customers, ask for product opinion, create discussion groups, etc. The best part is you do not have to pay anything.

- **Lead Generation** - Using social media, business owners can easily generate leads. Companies can use interesting content to attract new customers. If you focus on providing content your readers love to read, you will definitely get what you want.

- **Influencer Marketing** – Mostly business owners are familiar with this term. Some customers are persuasive and they simply spread the word about your products and services they actually love. This helps in building lots of customers. These people are basically influencing others and they are called influencers.

  Using social media, you can interact with these type of people on a daily basis. Any new message you want to spread among people can be done through influencers on social networking sites.

- **Follow-up** – Remain in contact with your existing customers by asking some casual questions. You can participate in discussions, respond to tweets, etc. This helps in solidifying your relationship with the existing customers and also helps in building new customers.

- **Online coupons and deals** – Keep on giving discount coupons and deals on networking sites to attract customers.

Following are the most popular Social Media Tools[7] used by businesses:

Graph 8.2

Chapter 9

Internet Videos for Small Businesses

Internet video is a great tool for promoting websites. Small business owners have to accept the truth, a single website cannot hit the customer's grand slam. They have to market their business using different means and methods, and one of the best is internet video. The main thing to be included in the video is the content and not the technology. Here are some of the best ways to use video marketing methods:

- **Show demos of products and services** – One of the best ways to promote your products and services is creating a video and place it on your website and YouTube (the best website for video marketing). Show how your products function, what else you can offer, etc. Show how your products and services provide a value to those who buy it.

- **New product launch** – This is almost the same as product demo, except you need to add a little extra juice to it as it is a new story. This is because this new product requires a detailed explanation of what the product does, how it works, and how it provides value to the purchaser. You can also include a press release for this new product launch, as well as a pre-launch marketing program.

- **Video Interviews** – This step most business owners forget to follow or take. An exclusive video interview is the best way to promote your new and existing products and services. This can be followed by some on the spot Testimonial Interview with new users.

  To create a video, all you need is a camcorder and start speaking in front of it. Here's the catch, anybody can speak in front of a camera, but do you think what is being said is actually interesting for the customers? It should and it must be interesting to potential buyers. It has to give them something of value – real or imaginary. Those people who are not in the habit of talking in front of a camera can come out with a dry and boring video with no interesting content for the buyer.

The best way to handle a video interview is to hire someone to ask questions and you answer the question in a relaxed manner. You can also edit the video and pause it at the right time before answering. This is not a live presentation or production. You can present anything in your videos about your business, products, services, future prospects, profits, etc.

The above are the best three ways of using videos, for business owners to promote their website and bring-in new customers.

Following is the chart showing percentage change in the use of Internet Videos and TV[8]:

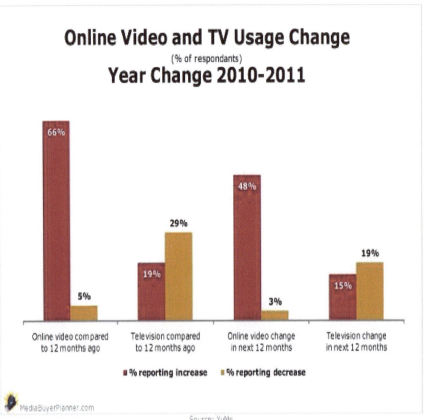

Chart 9.1

Chapter 10

Future in Mobile Marketing

In the past three years mobile marketing has grown to unbelievable heights. It has become the hottest topic of discussion for everybody, especially small businesses. By December 2009, 91% of the American population owned a mobile phone.

Right now what you are experiencing using your mobile device is just a beginning. Email, photos, video, social networking, etc., are just a beginning. There is much more you will see in the future. There is stuff coming you cannot even imagine today.

The best mobile marketing strategy small businesses are using today is text messaging. The responsiveness of a text message is more than 15 times when compared to email. At this time, the power of SMS can double the profits of local business and research has shown it will keep on increasing like crazy in the coming years.

Each year; not even a year, each day, you see new mobile applications being introduced and people are actually interested in these applications; especially the teens. The popularity of mobile applications is helping mobile marketing, which is helping businesses grow.

So which business will not use this strategy in future? The simple and straight answer is "EVERYONE WILL USE IT" or the business will DIE.

The internet and mobile phones have changed the world. Today, more than 83% of people in the world own a mobile phone and everything now seems to be revolving around this new technology.

Business owners know old marketing methods and old experts are not working. They are finding it is harder to grow their business and their expenses are increasing each day. They are slowly learning the world has changed. Each business owner needs to learn how the world has changed and what they need to do to change their business to not only survive but to grow. They need to realize marketing has shifted away from the methods used in the past, to newer marketing methods on the internet, mobile phones, and social media! This change / conversion will happen faster than any time in the past.

This change is already here!

The real question is, "Have you as a business owner made the change?"

If you don't change and your business doesn't change, you can guarantee your competition has or is about to change.

The capabilities of a mobile phone will keep on growing, and this minicomputer will present you with things which will surely be of a great help for you.

Here is the chart how business owners plan to Utilize Different Marketing Strategies in Future[9]: 🐭

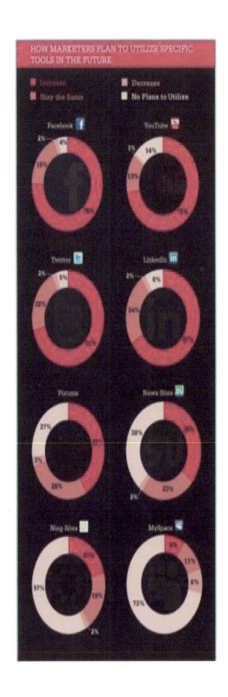

Chart 10.1

Chapter 11

Should You Outsource Your MobSoc?

"I am looking for a position in a company who wants to grow their business and increase their profits. I am a MobSoc (Mobile and Social) marketing expert. I will spend 85% of my time each day on MobSoc sites (Facebook, Twitter, Blogs, YouTube, SMS texting, etc.) promoting your company and products, and the remaining 15% of my time will be preparing the materials needed for the MobSoc sites."

Do you have an opening for this individual? Well, you should!

It's definitely a unique age we live in, where this kind of person just described has a bright future in MobSoc marketing. In fact, in all likelihood this type of person will be the next vital cog in your company's success machine, and more than likely, the success and the very survival of you company will depend upon how soon this type of person is working for your company.

How can this be, you ask?

Marketing Sherpa just released a new report showing an increasing trend in companies   outsourcing their MobSoc Marketing Responsibilities.

This is probably not the first time this comes to mind when you hear 'outsourcing', but it's a brilliant idea. MobSoc Marketing can seriously boost the brand and success of your company. Today, without MobSoc Marketing, companies can't get their feet off the ground, which will push business failure rates even higher.

Finding someone with a love and knack for MobSoc Marketing is a great opportunity for you to take your company to the next level.

If you and your company are not into MobSoc – Mobile Marketing and Social Media – Marketing, maybe you should consider a career change.   ❦

End Notes

1. Source: http://blog.junta42.com.php5-17.dfw1-2.websitetestlink.com/2010/03/mobile-marketing-stats-trends/mobile-content-marketing-stats/

2. Source: http://www.motomessage.com/mobile-marketing-ad-spending-statistics-predictions/

3. Source: http://www.marketingcharts.com/wp/wp-content/uploads/2009/11/campaigner-hurwitz-associates-very-small-business-use-marketing-tools-november-2009.jpg

4. Source: http://www.tec-it.com/pics/news/business_card.gif

5. Source:http://heidicohen.com/qr-code-data

6. Source: http://www.flowtown.com/blog/everybodys-doing-it-how-marketers-are-utilizing-social-media-in-2010

7. Source: http://www.flowtown.com/blog/everybodys-doing-it-how-marketers-are-utilizing-social-media-in-2011

8. Source:http://www.mediabuyerplanner.com/entry/81650/consumer-online-video-and-tv-usage-change-past-and-next-12-months/

9. Source: http://www.flowtown.com/blog/everybodys-doing-it-how-marketers-are-utilizing-social-media-in-2010

www.ingramcontent.com/pod-product-compliance
Lightning Source LLC
Chambersburg PA
CBHW041143050326
40689CB00001B/467